Love, Sex, & Karaoke:
52 ways to ignite your love life

Todd Creager

Love, Sex & Karaoke:
52 Ways to Ignite your Love Life

Todd Creager

Love, Sex & Karaoke:
52 WAYS TO IGNITE YOUR LOVE LIFE

Cover by: Ann Bennett Marketing

Copyright © 2015 Todd Creager
All rights reserved. No part of this book may be reproduced in any form by any electronic or mechanical means including photocopying, recording, or information storage and retrieval without permission in writing from the author.

ISBN-13: 978-0-692-37219-7

www.toddcreager.com
Email: contact@toddcreager.com

Give feedback on the book at:
feedback@toddcreager.com

Printed in U.S.A

To Cherie -
my lovely wife and soulmate of 30 years
who has taught me so much about what love is;
who has traveled with me through the many highs and
some lows, as our connection has deepened;
who has helped me find my own unique voice so that I
may love better and contribute more. As we embark on
our next stage of being empty-nesters with
both children away at college, it is wonderful to know
what I have to look forward to - a continued relationship
adventure filled with love, passion and play!

Contents

Introduction 1

Tip 1 4
Slow Down and Start Listening to the "Self"

Tip 2 6
This weekend, experiment with being your opposite.

Tip 3 8
Ask your partner what you can do or say to him (or her) this weekend that would thrill his/her soul.

Tip 4 10
Don't wait to be "in the mood" to be romantic.

Tip 5 12
Make this slow touch weekend...

Tip 6 14
Commit to Spending Quality Time with Your Partner this Weekend

Tip 7 16
Go Play Catch With Your Partner

Tip 8 18
If you want your partner to "catch your ball"...

You'd better catch theirs first.

Tip 9 20
The Relationship Between

Radical Self-Acceptance, Risk-Taking and a

Juicy Relationship

Tip 10 22
Ask some interesting and provocative questions this weekend and get to know your partner in a

deeper way

Tip 11 .... **24**
Find some new experience you could do as a couple this weekend.

Tip 12 .... **26**
This weekend be a more fulfilling partner.

Tip 13 .... **28**
Sometimes the problem is we do not say enough.

Tip 14 .... **30**
Activity List

Tip 15 .... **32**
Make sure you have time away from your lover.

Tip 16 .... **34**
Dependency is not a dirty word...

Tip 17

Let this be Forgiveness Weekend.

Tip 18 .... **38**
Start shifting your self-perceptions...

Tip 19 .... **40**
Start shifting your self-talk with this tool.

Tip 20 .... **42**
Do you want a great sex life? Then start talking!

Tip 21 .... **44**
How You Perceive Your Partner Changes Everything

Tip 22 .... **46**
This weekend, think of your most romantic moment

Tip 23 .... **48**
Dress up sexy and tell your partner it is all for him (or her).

Tip 24 50
Do something new and different for your mind, body and spirit.

Tip 25 52
Have you been too busy to take the time to be with your mate?

Tip 26 54
Which philosophy of life is closer to how you live?

Tip 27 56
Do something new and different in the bedroom (or the kitchen, or the rooftop) this weekend.

Be creative. Surprise him (or her).

Tip 28 58
Ask yourself - are you more of an inflamer or a shutting downer?

Tip 29 60
For Men Only

Tip 30 62
For Women Only

Tip 31 64
Make this an acceptance weekend.

Tip 32 66
Ask for negative feedback this weekend.

Tip 33 68
Practice disarming your partner this weekend.

Tip 34 70
This weekend try something totally different!

Tip 35 72
Take Time and Enjoy the View.

Tip 36 74
Take time to enjoy the rest of your senses as well.

Tip 37 76
I have decided this for you – yes this weekend is "enjoy being your sexual self with your partner weekend."

Tip 38 78
Help your partner weekend

Tip 39 80
Read a book to each other

Tip 40 82
Take time to explore

aspects of yourself and your partner.

Tip 41 84
Face a fear this weekend.

Tip 42 86
What are you sad about in your life?

What would you like to change?

Tip 43 88
Money and Relationship Bliss

Tip 44 90
Money and the Four Temperaments

Tip 45 92
Co-parenting & Showing a United Front

Tip 46 94
Live with gratitude especially looking for reasons to be grateful for your partner.

Tip 47 96
Let this be slow down and cuddle weekend.

Tip 48 98
This weekend, do something for your growth.

Tip 49 100
Let this be massage weekend.

Tip 50 102
Celebrate and Embrace Your Body

Tip 51 104
Use this weekend to go further out on a limb than ever before.

Tip 52 106
This weekend, splurge on a real romantic date.

Acknowledgements

I want to acknowledge two key people in my work life who have been essential to my career growth and success including the creation of this book.

One is Ann Bennett, a branding and marketing coach extraordinaire who has helped me not only in terms of financial success but also in helping me become more of my authentic self in my writing and in my speaking. I am glad she has been in my life these last three years.

The second person is Kristen Poborsky who Ann introduced me to, not too long after I met Ann. Kristen is my marketing strategist getting my message about sex and marital well-being out there to increasing numbers of people. She is reliable, consistent and has taken many burdens off my plate so that I can focus on my craft of helping couples and individuals have better lives and relationships.

I love having these two women on my team and am grateful for their involvement and friendship.

Introduction

Working with couples for over 30 years, you might think I would be jaded about committed, long-term relationships.

However, the opposite is true. I am very optimistic and excited about the future of intimate relationships.

Why? My optimism is based on the thousands of couples I have saved from divorce and tens of thousands I have helped, as well as my own long lasting marriage. What I am about to share with you are the same exact things I that I have done that has made my own marriage wildly satisfying and sexy for the past 30 years.

Our primary motivation as human beings is survival. We have learned to protect ourselves; not so much any more from physical harm, but instead from psychological harm. We protect our more vulnerable areas (i.e.- the parts of ourselves that are fearful, insecure, wounded) in a myriad of ways.

These ways include such behaviors such as:

1. fighting and bickering
2. physical or emotional withdrawal
3. excessive drug or alcohol use
4. other addictions such as food, sex and computer
5. infidelity

Here is the good news! By practicing the opposite of those self-protective tendencies, you can experience deeply satisfying love, pleasure and security in your relationship.

What seems like a miracle is totally doable. As you stay open instead of unconsciously closed, stay engaged, rather than detached and taking responsibility for the energy in your relationship amazing wonderful shifts begin to manifest a wildly satisfying sexy life.

Doing Karaoke requires to find and use your voice, stand out and make an impact, so people can enjoy your self expression. (And you don't have to be a great singer!)

It involves courage and it brings out the playful side of you. Creating a satisfying committed relationship can be a lot like singing karaoke.

My hope is that this book will help you find and use your voice to uplift your partner and others and to courageously and playfully live your life to your fullest capacity!

How to use this book

This book is a guide full of creative suggestions and ideas for YOU to manifest miracles in your relationship.

Every weekend, you can apply one of these suggestions to "ignite" your relationship so that you can have more love, more passion and more joy. As you open the book, on the left side will be a page with suggestions and thoughts for the upcoming weekend. On the right side will be a brief statement about the words on the previous page and your opportunity to write your own words to plan, motivate and inspire yourself into positive action. Utilize this book as a momentum builder. You can do the suggestions in the order in which they are written or you can bounce around and see what resonates with you for the upcoming weekend.

Thank you for purchasing this book!

As a special thank you for purchasing this book, I have created some additional resources for you which can be found here: http://toddcreager.com/bookbonus

There you will find additional tips and my free download: *7 Ways to Create a Wildly Satisfying Sexy Life*.

Enjoy the journey.

Enjoy your own growth process.

Enjoy having the love you want!

Todd Creager

Tip 1
Slow Down and Start Listening to the "Self"

This is the number 1 thIng we DON'T DO. Society runs in fast motion, we have a lot to do and allow technology to eat up our free time. This takes a toll on our lives and relationships.

There is much going on "out there" but there also is much going on "in here."

Periodic slowing down to listen to ourselves actually makes us more effective and we get more done. Listening to "self" means developing a receptive state of mind which allows you to enjoy smelling the roses, hearing birds chirping, tasting delicious food, feeling the gentle wind across your face and seeing a cute baby's smile.

Tuning in your senses reanimates the world around you. It is a more soulful way to live.

Slow down for periods of the day to experience your own bodily emotions, sensations and desires. And utilize this same receptive state of mind to become a good listener to others. Most people spend very little time listening with full attention is on the other person, taking in what they are saying, meaning and feeling.

One of the great joys is to have the experience of being heard even if what needs to be heard are unpleasant, difficult feelings and opinions.

Couples waste so much time trying to prove their respective points and push their own agendas. When you slow down and become receptive; you have more of what you want from you partner.

Commit to a daily dose of slowing down. Do a simple breathing meditation or simply ask yourself what you are feeling right now. Develop a receptive state of mind.

Use the same receptive state of mind to practice being a truly effective listener and see how quickly your relationships improve.

Tip 1

Write down some times for the week where you plan to listen to yourself. When we schedule things, we do them; when we don't schedule things, we typically don't.

Also, write down some of things you notice about yourself when you slow down and become receptive.

Tip 2
This weekend, experiment with being your opposite.

If you are sexually conservative, do an erotic dance for your partner. Let him be surprised; let him squirm; let him be delighted.

Whatever his or her response is, go for it.
Life is about experimenting and relationships are most definitely about experimenting.

If you tend to be egocentric, spend the entire weekend focusing on the wellbeing of your partner and other loved ones.

If you are a leader, follow your partner's lead. If you are a follower, plan a date or an outing.

Yes, be your opposite and you may find out that the opposite of you is also you.

Tip 2

Make 2 short columns. On the left side jot down a few of your tendencies. On the right side, write down the opposite of those tendencies. Pick one of your opposites and commit to manifesting your opposite this weekend. Write down a few things you will do or say to express that recessive part of you.

Tip 3
Ask your partner what you can do or say to him (or her) this weekend that would thrill his/her soul.

What would elevate your partner's energy? Be an impact partner and do it if it is at all possible.

If it is not possible, ask for something that would be possible. Sometimes a partner may have difficulty coming up with something.

Don't give up...

Keep on your partner until you get an answer. Then follow through. You are far more interpersonally powerful than you think!

Tip 3

Write down a few things you can do or say that would uplift your partner. If you ask her or him what would be uplifting, write them down here as well.

Tip 4
Don't wait to be "in the mood" to be romantic.

There are certain things that I need to do that if I waited to be "in the mood" I might do it every February 29th! Or never!

Be romantic this weekend.

All it takes to be romantic is to:

1. Decide that you are that person who can lift the spirit of your partner.
2. Visualize the smile on your partner's face when she is the recipient of your romantic gesture.
3. Then do it!

Even if you're not "in the mood," your mood will probably change after you behave as the Casanova you latently are!

Tip 4

Think about times you have done things when you were not in the mood that gave you significant benefits and write them down. Inspire yourself to overcome your resistance to be romantic.

Tip 5
Make this slow touch weekend...

Touch your partner as if she (or he) is the most precious and cherished and treasured person in the world.

You want your touch to leave your partner feeling loved, cherished, admired, appreciated, special, significant and beautiful (or handsome).

Tip 5

Imagine doing that slow touch. See you and your partner as if you are in a romantic movie together. Then be in your own body in the movie and notice how it feels to have those slow hands. Feel free to write down any thoughts, feelings or resistances as you imagine this.

Tip 6
Commit to Spending Quality Time with Your Partner this Weekend

Take the number of hours you worked this week (if you are a stay at home mother or volunteer-you can still look at your time that you give to others as work time). Divide that number by 10 and commit to giving that amount (or more) of QUALITY time to your partner this weekend. If you worked 40 hours, make sure that you give 4 quality hours to your partner.

Quality time spent means time focused on the other person. Watching a movie does not count; it has to be interactional time.

Here are some ideas to get you started:

- Go out to dinner and talk with your partner
- Take a walk or hike together
- Make Love
- Sit and gaze into each other's eyes
- Cuddle or engage in any mutually enjoyable activity where there is some exchange of intimate or playful energy.

Talking about vacation plans or problems with the children is not quality time; while it is important time it isn't about focusing on your partner. Make suggestions and ask your partner what he/she wants to do this weekend. Then **find something to do during your quality time that will lead you both to getting closer, feeling sexier and more filled up.**

Tip 6

Make a calendar for the week as you set aside 10% of the time you devote to "work" or other pursuits to your intimate partner. Write down what you will do this week and over the next month. You could borrow from my list or think of something else.

Tip 7
Go Play Catch With Your Partner

Want to stop letting emotional pain come between you and your partner?

Want to turn a cold relationship into a hot one?

Then learn to play catch!

Do you remember the last time you played catch? If you threw the ball and the other person caught it, you had a satisfied feeling. If the other person just watched the ball hit the ground after you threw it to him, It would feel very unsatisfying.

Relationships never break up because of emotional pain, they break up because partners feel disconnected.

If you are a partner in an intimate relationship, you need to think differently about pain, especially when your partner is angry or disappointed with you. Learn to accept it and don't fight it.

Play catch with your partner and shift to a receptive state of mind so you can receive your partner's pain.

- Give up trying to change your partner's mind.
- Give up trying to prove you're right.
- Relax and take in WHATEVER your partner is expressing to you.

Your turn will come!

Tip 7

1. Write down some feelings, thoughts or desires that you would like to say to your partner.

2. Write down some feelings, thoughts or desires that your partner has tried expressing to you that you have been defensive about. Notice your feelings and resistances to listening and commit yourself to be receptive to your partner about these things.

Tip 8
If you want your partner to "catch your ball"...
You'd better catch theirs first.

**If you want your partner to "catch your ball"...
You'd better catch theirs first.**

Trust this process. Ask yourself- "How much has it benefited me in the past to interrupt him/her; to disagree or correct him/her before he/she felt heard and understood?" The answer to that question is it has it helped you at all? **You can learn how to be receptive and get more of what you want from your partner.**

Try something new even if it takes some patience and discipline

See your partner as an ally, even when you are angry and you will more easily bring out the listener in him/her. Don't yell or get overly critical; that's like throwing the ball too hard for the other person to catch it.

Here's an example:
Partner 1: I am so angry with you. You did not remember to do the one thing I asked you to do for me.

Partner 2: *(puts aside his defensive reaction, takes a deep breath and exhales)* Yeah- I could see it on your face how angry you are. I don't blame you; you really needed me to come through for you and I didn't. Is there anything else you need to express to me?

Partner 1: (A little less angry) I just feel let down.

Partner 2: Yes- I know.

Partner 1: All right, well please remember next time.

Partner 2: I'll write it down and put it on the refrigerator next time.

Partner 1: OK- Thanks.

Tip 8

Write a script of a past dialogue that went awry with your partner but THIS TIME- the script demonstrates clean communication and a healthy game of catch.

Tip 9
The Relationship Between Radical Self-Acceptance, Risk-Taking and a Juicy Relationship

Relationships are not for the faint of heart. As you practice radical self-acceptance, which is taking the position that you are ok no matter what the reaction of others including your intimate partner, you are free to take more risks.

For example: you are free to express what you feel or want, take more initiative, be more vulnerable, try a new sexual approach or show a new side of yourself. There is less at stake if you are judged or rejected because you know that no matter what, you accept yourself.

Decide to practice radical self-acceptance and take some chances; surprise your partner. The downside is usually negligible or non-existent. The upside is that you reinvigorate your relationship. This consistent leaving your comfort zone leads to freshness, novelty and stimulation for both partners.

Why have a dry, deadened relationship when you can be creative, take some interpersonal chances and have a juicy, alive relationship?

Choose radical self-acceptance and courage.

Tip 9

What are you holding back from or afraid to do with your partner because you are avoiding a possible negative outcome? Realize that what you are avoiding is your own inner critic. Make a vow to yourself that NO MATTER WHAT THE OUTCOME, you will accept yourself. Once you truly make that vow, you are now in a position to do take that risk or really do anything you want to do. Write about i tand your bold intentions here.

Tip 10
Ask some interesting and provocative questions this weekend and get to know your partner in a deeper way

Here are some examples to help you start asking:

"What is something about you that few if any people know about because you are afraid that if they found out, you would be embarrassed? "

"What is a sexual fantasy of yours?"

"If you had to live your life over again- what would you do differently or the same?"

There are many questions that could bring out something deeper within your partner that you could ask.

Asking these types of questions will help lead you to a more open, closer and intimate experience as a couple.

Tip 10

In the spirit of developing your own healthy curiosity, jot down some questions here you can ask your partner to deepen the connection between you both. Also write some questions you would like to be asked by your partner to you!

Tip 11
Find some new experience you could do as a couple this weekend.

Here are three examples to get you thinking about trying something new:

Find a social dance class, don't worry about how good a dancer you are.

Go to a karaoke bar and sing a duet together, don't worry about how good a singer you are.

Rent a kayak for two, don't worry about if you don't know how to kayak.

Whatever you choose to do with your partner this weekend, get comfortable with stretching past your comfort zone.

It's good for you and your relationship to stretch and get out of routines.

If you end up liking what you did, you can do it again or take a class. My wife and I suggested that a couple start taking western swing classes years ago and now they are consistently the US Open champions in swing for the 50 and over crowd. We are now taking dance lessons from them. So you may even find some undiscovered skill. And if you don't, then be like the rest of us and just **enjoy new dimensions of experience with your partner.**

Tip 11

Share this suggestion with your partner and together write down some ideas of new activites you could do immediately, in the short term and in the long term. Make them happen!

Tip 12
This weekend be a more fulfilling partner.

Here's a little clue: What is the trait about your partner that is the most irritating?

In most cases, whatever that trait is- is the very trait you need to develop MORE OF IN YOURSELF!

For example:

If your partner is too "irresponsible", you may be overly responsible and need to be more playful and silly and less of a "manager."

Or, if you're partner is too "anal," it may mean that you need to pay more attention to your own clutter and clean some things up.

This works with our children as well. The traits that bug us about our children may also point to areas of ourselves that need more developing and attention.

The thing that most attracted us to our partners at first later can drive us crazy. You may have liked that wild, crazy person you were dating; only now that you married him, you are tired of his irresponsibility. We are attracted to people often times because they are manifesting what is hidden or latent in ourselves.

When I have seen a partner practice this, the other partner often changes as well and in a direction that is desirable.

Try this and see what happens!

Tip 12

What about your partner is irritating or drives you crazy? Does my "clue" fit here? Do you have a lack of this trait or dimension in yourself? Promise yourself that you will develop this quality in yoursef and take action in that direction. Write about it and notice any changes tha subsequently happen in your spouse.

Tip 13
Sometimes the problem is we do not say enough.

When your partner expresses something where he or she is in some sort of emotional pain, get specific about what it is like for her or him. In other words, use words to let your lover know that you understand where they are coming from.

Here are 3 samples of communication; one is unproductive and provocative, the second is far better and ok but the third is far more impactful.

Example #1:
Partner 1: I am so hurt that you once again did not listen to me and went right to you and your stuff.
Partner 2: Well, you're not the only one that is upset!

Example #2:
Partner 1: I am so hurt that you once again did not listen to me and went right to you and your stuff.
Partner 2: I hear that you are so hurt.

Example #3:
Partner 1: I am so hurt that you once again did not listen to me and went right to you and your stuff.
Partner 2: Yes, I hear that you are very hurt and that instead of staying with what was bothering you, I went to me. I do that way too much and I can see how painful that is for you. I am truly sorry.

If you were Partner 1, how would example # 3 impact you?

Tip 13

Write down a few past scripts of difficult dialogues but end them differently this time. Have your partner express some pain and this time you respond as in example # 3 above. Writing these scripts with you responding more impactfully will actually give you prwactice so that in the heat of the next difficult moment, you can be far more effective. You will find that when you do that response, pain dissolves quickly and the two of you become closer.

Tip 14
Activity List

Here are some free activities you can do with your spouse today or this weekend (or any day) to add some bliss you're your relationship:

1. Take a walk around your neighborhood and don't forget to hold hands and do other PDA's (public display of affection)
2. Put on some music and ask your partner to dance.
3. Put on some music and ask your partner to sing.
4. Take a long shower together. (One long shower will not significantly raise your water bill)!
5. Hold hands and skip down the street together.
6. Cook a fancy meal of your choice together.
7. Decide to do something that usually is not of any interest of you but is of total interest to your partner. (i.e.-If you have a sports loving partner, do or watch that activity with him or her).
8. Have a picnic in a park for two.
9. Go hike in nature with each other.
10. Spend a day at the beach.
11. Finger-paint together.
12. Watch a movie you already have at home and make sure to sit close to each other.
13. Lie under the stars and see if you can find any constellations.
14. Do a bike ride together.
15. Last but not least- plan a day where you don't leave the bedroom except to eat.

Tip 14

Write down your top 3 choices either from this list or from your own set of ideas.

Tip 15
Make sure you have time away from your lover.

Develop your own separate interests. I remember a famous writer once said, "In my relationship, I want two things- I want passion and I want solitude"!

I do believe that having your own space for quiet time and doing your own activities gives you that sense of "I- ness" that is so important for embracing the "we-ness" of doing things together.

So enjoy your time alone AND your time together.

Tip 15

Ask yourself this question. "Do I have a sense of my own individuality in my relationship?" If you do, great- what do you do to maintain your own important sense of "separateness": from your partner. If you do not, start making a list of separate activities you could do or people you can spend time with (appropriately).

Tip 16
Dependency is not a dirty word...

As Barbara Streisand sings "People Who Need People Are the Luckiest People in the World." Being overly dependent and lacking self sufficiency is not what we are talking about here. However, we need to allow others to nourish us; give us love and pleasure. Probably and hopefully you do not need your partner to survive; but you do need your partner to thrive.

Ask yourself what you would like to have from or experience with your partner.

Be courageous enough to be vulnerable. If you have trouble with experiencing this healthy kind of dependency, seek a qualified expert to help you overcome this limitation.

The more vulnerable you allow yourself to be, the more bliss you will experience in your relationship.

Tip 16

Think out of your typical box on this one. What would make you thrive? More specifically, how could your spouse help you thrive? What is something you could ask of your partner that would be great if you received it?

Tip 17
Let this be Forgiveness Weekend.

Do you have someone to forgive including your lover this weekend? Forgiveness benefits the forgiver because it opens up the life flow inside the forgiver so that more bliss can be experienced. Holding on to past hurts create restrictions to joy and constrictions in your energy field.
Letting go of past hurts and angers allow for more positive change in the present and future.

One important aspect of forgiveness is to recalculate the intentions behind the negative behaviors of your partner (or someone else) when he or she did hurt you. More times than not, the partner was immature or protecting him or herself as opposed to having a true intention to hurt you. However, this is not an excuse.
Forgiveness paves the way for deeper understanding.

Forgiving someone does not give the other permission to continue treating you badly. Take care of yourself, set boundaries and open up to your partner in love and courage.

Tip 17

How have you been hurt in the past by your partner? Is there something that is particularly difficult to let go of? If there is, what is the most benign way of looking at why your partner did that to you? Remember, this is not to make an excuse for your partner's hurtful behavior but you want to open up to the possibility of moving past the hurt and having more life energy between the two of you.

Tip 18
Start shifting your self-perceptions...

If you have read my book, "The Long, Hot Marriage," you know I discuss the importance of shifting perceptions of your partner. But shifting self- perceptions are just as important. What are your automatic perceptions of yourself? Do you think of yourself as fun or boring? Successful or unsuccessful? Sexy or not sexy? Attractive or unattractive? In order to increase relationship bliss it always starts with your relationship with yourself.

Did you know that you can choose the self-perceptions you want?
Do you want to feel attractive? Or sexy or successful or sexy? You can. Next week, I go into detail about how you can change your self- perception. But here's the main thing. PRETEND until you believe it. Your automatic self-perceptions do not have to run you. Stretch into new perceptions even if it feels weird at first. Do not base your perceptions on history; that will just limit you.

Decide, practice and start being the person you want to be.

Tip 18

Really have fun with this one; play with it. First pretend just to yourself; maybe acting a new way in front of a mirror. Then tell your partner what you are up to and ask your partner to be a "teammate" in this stretching of yours. Enjoy pretending because you just may discover some other aspect of yourself you didn't know very well before.

Tip 19
Start shifting your self-talk with this tool.

Last week's Thursday tip discussed the importance of shifting self-perception and the importance of pretending to bring out these desired traits and self-perceptions.

Today I discuss a tool that I have used for many years that has led to deep change in people. WAFIT! WAFIT is a tool that if used correctly, will sure improve your life significantly.

WAFIT stands for Words, Actions, Feelings, Images and Thoughts.

Go to the following URL on your computer to learn more about the WAFIT: http://toddcreager.com/working-wafit-success-magnet/. I will tell you exactly how to use it to improve your life and relationship.

Now I want you to grab a piece of paper and honestly write down your automatic self-talk that gets in your way of having the life or relationship you want.

Think about these questions as you write:

Is your self-talk critical?

Do you scare yourself as you brace for a negative future?

Write down what you say to yourself and even others. Then write down how you act, feel, imagine (i.e.- what is your mental picture) and think. This automatic WAFIT creates a belief; sometimes a negative self-limiting one.

Now think of a belief you want to have

Write it down. **What would be the WAFIT you need to create to support this belief?** For example, what would you be saying to yourself? How would you act? Etc. Then practice "Conscious WAFITING" and see how your life takes shape!

Tip 19

Another variation on what I suggested above is to make 2 columns; title one 'automatic' WAFIT and the other 'conscious WAFIT. Then write W-on the left and write down your automatic self talk. Do the same for A(ctions), F(eelings),I(mages) and T(houghts). On the bottom, write down the negative belief that this automatic WAFIT leads to such as "I am a failure" or "I am unworthy". On the rights side, write down the positive flip side of that negative belief and begin filling out the conscious WAFIT above it that would support the belief you want to believe.THEN START LIVING OUT YOUR CONSCIOUS WAFIT!

Tip 20
Do you want a great sex life? Then start talking!

Do you want a great sex life? Then start talking!

If you want to heat up your relationship, I recommend that you develop three key skills:

- Communicate more impactfully and healthily with your partner
- Become less reactive and more creative
- Stay open when your reflex is to close or fight

Learning these skills leads to a more robust sex life.

As a couple learns how to have effective conversations, her heart opens up and dare I say- her vagina may follow. Men benefit from effective dialogues where both people get to express what they feel and want and both get the experience of being heard and understood.

A key to be a great expresser- See your partner as an ally.

Speak your feelings and desires with the mindset that your partner cares deeply for you. By doing this you will encourage your partner's abilities to listen and pay attention.

A key to be a great listener- Practice a receptive state of mind.

Think of the last time you were in nature and just took in the sounds, sights and smells. That is a receptive state of mind. Now imagine doing that when your partner is expressing something to you; have no agenda and no particular goal. Just take in your partner's inner experience.

Tip 20

Write down how you would state your feelings or desires to your partner if you had the conscious mindset that he or she is an ally. If you had a dialogue recently that had a poor outcome, redo the dialogue on this paper with this new mindset.

Also, write down the experience you were thinking about when you were in a receptive state of mind. Memorize how your body feels from head to toe when you are having this receptive experience. Practice feeling this way more around your partner.

Tip 21
How You Perceive Your Partner Changes Everything

What are your perceptions of your partner both positive and negative? How you perceive a person makes it easier for him or her to become that. We underestimate the power of our perceptions and how much they can become self-fulfilling prophecies.

Examples Of Negative Perceptions That Lead To Self-Fulfilling Prophecies
- My partner is a poor listener.
- My partner cannot handle money.
- My partner will cheat on me.
- My partner is too serious.
- My partner is too controlling.
- My partner is sexually inhibited.

How to bring the best out of your partner:

1. Imagine your partner to have more of the traits that you wish for. How would you talk to, look at, ask of, or touch him/her? Experiment with talking, looking, asking, and touching him/her as you visualized.

2. Ask yourself, "What do I need to bring out of myself that is new and different that would make it easier for my partner to be more of what I want him/her to be? If you want your partner to be more accepting, maybe you need to be a better listener. Become that listening person and see how that changes their behavior.

3. If your relationship is stuck in a rut where there is distance and/or resentment, announce that YOU have been stuck in a rut. Tell him/her that YOU forgot how handsome, beautiful, wonderful...he/she is because of how you have been feeling. Show your love through an embrace or gentle touch.

Do not wait to "feel" like doing this. And definitely do not wait for your partner to perceive you differently or treat you better.

Tip 21

On this page, write down some of the things you were thinking of while reading this tip.

Tip 22
This weekend, think of your most romantic moment

Think about it... it may be the time when you swept your partner off her or his feet; where you blew him or her away.

It doesn't matter if it was last week or 30 years ago...

Just take a big breath, relax and remember it as deeply as you can. Know that inside of you is that romantic person waiting to reappear. Break through any resistance you might be feeling to manifest that part of you this weekend.

No excuses, don't wait to be in the mood.

Break free, break from the monotony and the status quo. Don't worry about how it ends up or even how your partner reacts to your romantic gesture, idea or initiation. Just give your partner something wonderful to respond to.

And if your partner is uncomfortable with it, so be it. Make your partner squirm. It is for a good cause!

Tip 22

Write about one of the times in your relationship history when you blew your partner away. Then commit to writing what you will do to blow him or her away this weekend.

Tip 23
Dress up sexy and tell your partner it is all for him (or her).

Dress to impress and arouse. And don't say you will do it when your body is better or perfect or whatever. If you do not have clothes that flatter you, go buy some. The time is now to celebrate your sexiness with your partner.

Remember that sexiness is a state of mind more than anything.

Tip 23

This is your page to make affirmations about how sexy you are. Examples could be something simple like "I am sexy" to something more specific such as "I am sexy in the dress I will put on for him this evening."

Tip 24
Do something new and different for your mind, body and spirit.

Self care leads to greater health, wealth and the ability to give and receive love.

- Do Yoga. (There seems to be a Yoga Center on every corner and most fitness centers have classes as well).
- Learn to meditate.
- Do a new and fun kind of exercise or workout.
- Start a hobby you have been thinking about doing.
- Life is an adventure.

Be open to it especially in ways that quiet your mind, increase the health of your body and lift your spirit.

Tip 24

List one thing you will do that can quiet your mind, one that is specifically good for your body and one that can enliven your spirit. Commit to at least one item on your list this week.

Tip 25
Have you been too busy to take the time to be with your mate?

Decide to create a sense of urgency to be with him or her. Drop everything for 10- 20 minutes or more.

I mean DROP EVERYTHING and TOTALLY FOCUS ON YOUR LOVER.

Your to-do list will still be waiting. Your football game will be waiting. Your e-mail will be waiting. Just make sure your partner doesn't wait.

As they say, 10-quality attention- focused minutes a day keeps the divorce attorney away!

Tip 25

On a scale of 1-10, rate the quality of your emotional connection to your partner before doing this exercise. After 3 consecutive days of doing the 10-20 minute exercise with your partner, come back to this page and rate the quality of your emotional connection again. If it went up, of course keep doing it. If it stayed the same or went down, ask each other what may be contributing to this. Almost all the time, that number will go up!

Tip 26
Which philosophy of life is closer to how you live?

1. **Life is about being comfortable as much as possible and to avoid problems and challenges.**
2. **Life is about leaning past your comfort zone consistently to open up to more of life's energy and to expand and grow.**

If you chose number one, I would suggest making another choice! Living life with philosophy number two is the only way that I see to be truly happy in life.

Now with relationships, this is double true!

You know you want a joyful, satisfying relationship. Then apply philosophy number two; don't just like the sound of it, live it! Lean past your comfort zone and know that on the other side of discomfort, problems and uncomfortable feelings is joy and passion. Decide to feel and stay open.
Before Mervyns' closed, there would always be that silly commercial at this time of year with a woman standing at the door of Mervyns' before the time it is supposed to open and she is looking in and saying the same words I want to say to you...

"Open, open, open!"

Tip 26

What is the first thought that comes to your mind when asked to leave your comfort zone? If it is a fear based thought, just notice it and decide to not let it control or limit you. Then write down the first 3 things that come to mind that you can do that would symbolize leaving your comfort zone and opening up to more life and more love.

Tip 27
Do something new and different in the bedroom (or the kitchen, or the rooftop) this weekend. Be creative. Surprise him (or her).

If you are afraid this new behavior will "freak" your partner out, let your partner know that you want to stretch yourself a little bit and be more stimulating and interesting. This will give your partner a heads up.

Those of you that are familiar with my work and thinking know that **I totally believe that the best intimate relationships are those that allow for newness and experimentation.** If you do this experimentation enough, then the "new" is expected and you may not even need to give your partner a heads up.

Tip 27

Continuing the theme of leaving your comfort zone, write down what you plan on doing. If you have trouble thinking of something, google-"things to do to surprise my spouse" or some version of that. Or ask friends or read Cosmopolitan.

Tip 28
Ask yourself - are you more of an inflamer or a shutting downer?

An inflamer tends to get agitated when upset, raise one's voice, get anxious, get aggressive, talk faster, etc. The inflamer may externalize his or her upset or anxiety and put others on the defensive.

A shutting downer tends to withdraw, get quiet, numb oneself with TV or computer, stonewall and/or avoids. He or she internalizes his stress or finds a way to not feel it. ("I feel fine" is a common sentence of a shutting downer who does not reveal a whole lot about his or her inner life).

If you are an inflamer, try practicing self-soothing activities such as deep breathing, meditation, self-soothing internal dialogue, muscle relaxation exercises and physical activity.

If you are a shutting downer, try connecting with yourself and your partner. Locate your inner feelings, look deeply into your partner's eyes (to see if feelings emerge), express feelings of all kinds (both pleasant and unpleasant), seek a support group and practice imagining your heart area opening up.

A good therapist or coach can help both kinds of people reach these goals. I have seen many partners change their lives for the better when they did what they could to turn off these automatic responses that were keeping them stuck.

Tip 28

Are you more of an inflamer or shutting downer? You might want to write down of there is anyone on your family of origin you take after in this respect. Write down how this role model's reactive behavior deterred him or her from having the relationship that was possible. Also, write down what YOU are willing to do to stop that trend and feel free to take suggestions from the words on the left page.

Tip 29
For Men Only

Be masculine this weekend. What does that mean? My definition of masculinity is it is that part of you that can make things happen, affect others positively and penetrate her world in loving, helpful ways. Your masculinity evokes your partner's femininity. When you are masculine, she opens up and receives and allows you to penetrate her world. She receives your loving gestures and words and opens her heart and body in trust and receptivity. So what are some masculine things you can do?

Be a great listener. Listen to her complaints about you; that's right- listen to her complaints and feelings and stay interested; do not get defensive. As difficult as that is for most of us men, it is the most masculine thing you can do because it inspires her trust and openness.

Here are a couple of suggestions to get you started:

Plan a date.

Initiate lovemaking.

Ask her how you can help take one task off her plate. (Very masculine!)

Touch her with the intention to make her feel more loved than ever.

Tip 29

Practice imagining your wife or girlfriend complain about you to you and feel yourself stay open and non-defensive as you listen to her experience of you (whether you agree or not is irrelevant). When you feel ready, ask her to reveal a problem she has with you with the promise that you will be interested, accepting and non-defensive. Also, write down what else you would be willing to do to evoke her femininity.

Tip 30
For Women Only

Be feminine this weekend.

1. Take the time to stop. Take time for you.
2. Allow your man to do something for you. Ask him to please you. Ask him to do you a favor.
3. No matter what the history of your relationship has been, see him as a person who cares about you and treat him that way. Treat him as someone you can count on. In some relationships and in some areas of life, that may be too difficult if there have been reasons to distrust. But do your best to find the things that are trustworthy about your partner.
4. And sexually, make sure that you know and he knows that your pleasure is important. Take in his love as imperfect as his love may be. Find ways to enjoy him. Lay in his lap and let him caress you. Put your head on his shoulder and let him hold you. Be willing to be vulnerable; at least as much as you can.

Tip 30

Write down here that you are committed to taking some time for yourself daily even if it is as little as 10 minutes! Also, write down what you are willing to ask of him this week. Lastly, write down the times he has come through for you and allowed you to feel safe and vulnerable even if it has been a while ago

Tip 31
Make this an acceptance weekend.

Practice accepting something about yourself and also accept something about your partner that you have had resistance to accepting. Of course I am not asking you to accept poor treatment or abuse. I am talking about something you are critical about yourself or your partner and that you just give it a rest for the weekend.

It is truly amazing how much positive impact we have over our mental and physical health by shifting from judgmental to accepting. Our muscles relax, our blood pressure lowers and we often act in ways that is so appealing to others that they often act in ways that then make our lives even better.

Tip 31

Make 2 columns. Make the right column wider than the left. On the left column write what you are critical of yourself and/or your partner. On the right column, write an accepting statement. For example- on the left you might write- Weight gain. On the right column, you write- I accept my body as it is and will do what I need to reach my body goals.

Tip 32
Ask for negative feedback this weekend.

You're saying – "What? ASK for negative feedback? Are you asking me to be a masochist"?

No – it is actually a great thing to do that could help two people – you and your lover. How does it help you?

It gets you to practice a concept I call "Radical Self Acceptance."

One of the greatest things I have learned is the importance of being ok with negative feedback. It gives me the opportunity to practice accepting myself no matter what and also improving. I do that every semester as a USC instructor. My graduate students tell me how I can teach better. I think it is great. And they love it. They love that they feel heard and important. I get high ratings every semester and I think my openness is one of the biggest factors.

Likewise, your partner will love it too.

Like my students, your partner will feel significant and cared about. Be interested in her or his negative feedback. If you get defense, it is because you are thinking about negative feedback incorrectly. Negative feedback is an opportunity to learn about yourself and your partner.

So ask for negative feedback this weekend and make it a habit. It works miracles. Try it and let me know how it works for you and your relationship.

Tip 32

Think of the three main issues that your partner brings up that is negative about you and write them down. Commit to practicing radical self acceptance and ask your partner to express those items to you and that THIS TIME you will totally listen and be receptive and empathetic.

Tip 33
Practice disarming your partner this weekend.

Disarming is mainly comprised of 2 things:
1. Look for the truth in what your partner is saying, even if it seems mostly untrue or unfair.
2. Own up to as much of your contribution to the problem as you can.

Here is an example of an ineffective listening:

Partner 1: You have not asked me out for a date for what seems like forever. I guess you don't enjoy my company anymore.

Partner 2: That's you. Always focusing on what I don't do rather than what I do for you. Did you forget that I have been under a lot of work stress? And what about the date I arranged 6 weeks ago?

Here is an example of disarming:

Partner 1: You have not asked me out for a date for what seems like forever. I guess you don't enjoy my company anymore.

Partner 2: You are right. It has been a long time since I have asked you out, maybe as much as 6 weeks ago and that is way too long.

I have been under a lot of work stress but I could have made time for you somewhere in there. I apologize for not paying attention enough to you.

Disarming is POWERFUL and it works. Nobody loses, everybody wins! So practice disarming and have a wonderful weekend. I am sure you will!

Tip 33

Like last week's tip, when you practice this suggestion it will build your "emotional muscle." Think of something your partner has said over time that is negative about you that you have not fully taken responsibility. Look for the truth in your partner's statement. (Practice radical self acceptance). Write down the negative truth about yourself (Don't worry, you are still ok as a person, except a little more mature and a little more ready to have a great relationship). If you are up for it, write down two more. Then plan on going up to your partner and owning up to that issue.

Tip 34
This weekend try something totally different!

This is one of those weekends where you can choose to do something totally different with your partner that you both have not done for a long time or have never done.
What is that activity?

Give it some thought and initiate.

If at first your partner says no, tell him or her how important it is to you to have this adventure or do this activity with him or her. If there is a positive response, great! If not, see if there is a compromise. If it does not happen, know that at least you went for it.

Tip 34

Jot down as many ideas as you can think of that you will ask your partner.

Tip 35
Take Time and Enjoy the View.

Focus on as many of the 5 senses as you can this weekend when with your partner or even if by yourself. We often get too much in our heads and miss experiencing what is right in front of us.

Use your sense of vision and see the beauty around you:
Did you miss the plants that are in your house or in your backyard?
Or how about the green leaves of the trees outside your window with the backdrop of the blue sky?

How about enjoying looking at the smile of your spouse or children?

You don't have to go very far to take in the visual beauty around you. And of course, if you are in a relationship enjoy the look of your partner's body even if it is not perfect.

Tip 35

Write down how it was for you to focus on one the beauty around you and allow yourself to enjoy the moment.

Tip 36
Take time to enjoy the rest of your senses as well.

Pay attention to the sounds around you.
- Listen to music you like and really enjoy it; take it in.
- Enjoy taking in the sounds of nature or the sounds of your kids playing or talking.

Pay attention to your food more when you eat it.
- Too many of us eat way too fast. Slow down and chew slowly, take the time to enjoy tasting every bite.

Enjoy the smells and aromas around you.
- The smell of your soap or shampoo.
- The particular scent of your spouse.
- The smells of cooking in your kitchen or the smells of nature.

Enjoy touching and being touched.
- Notice how it feels to touch or be touched by your spouse.
- Notice how it feels to feel warm water on your hands.

And of course, notice how you feel emotionally throughout the day. As you slow down your mind and notice the world around you through your five senses, you become more alive and more present.

Tip 36

Write about several sensual experiences you had with these variety of senses. What did you notice more deeply if anything? Was it enjoyable? Would you be willing to practice paying attention to your senses more often?

Tip 37
I have decided this for you – yes this weekend is "enjoy being your sexual self with your partner weekend."

Stretch here beyond your comfort zone. If you already are comfortable sexually, do something new, be a tease (not mean-spirited though). If you are relatively conservative, stretch yourself to a level beyond your comfort zone but not too much.

I will elaborate here:
There are three main modalities of foreplay: verbal foreplay, behavioral foreplay and non-verbal foreplay.

Examples of verbal foreplay:

- Expressions of appreciation and/or compliments
- Expressions of love, desire and caring
- Letting the person know earlier in the day of later sexual plans
- Asking partner what his or her sexual preference of the moment is

Examples of behavioral foreplay:
- Sending complimentary or sexual texts in the middle of the work day
- Hugging, kissing and soft gentle caress
- Increasing arousal through more sexual touch
- Teasing, sexual play

Examples of non-verbal foreplay:
- Smiling admiringly
- Longer eye gaze
- Other nonverbal facial expressions indicating approval or desire

Tip 37

Write down here any fears or resistances you have to this suggestion. Then ask yourself "What is the worst thing that can happen, really?" Be willing to risk it. After you stretch your sexual self with your partner, write down how that experience was for you.

Tip 38
Help your partner weekend

This week's tip is short, sweet and very powerful when you practice it!

Help a partner out this weekend. Go out of your way to be kind. Be more cooperative than usual; be a team player. Ask what you could do to make the weekend more pleasurable or less stressful.

Tip 38

Write down what you did and how it felt afterward.

Tip 39
Read a book to each other

Read a good relationship book to each other this weekend. Take turns reading out loud.

I highly recommend my book: **The Long Hot Marriage** and you can find it on my website if you do not own a copy: http://toddcreager.com/store/

Tip 39

Write down how that experience was for you and your partner.

Tip 40
Take time to explore
aspects of yourself and your partner.

What's great about marriage is the potential for two partners to use the committed relationship to explore aspects of each other and themselves.

The sexual arena can be a great area to discover and play with many aspects of ourselves. Being fully alive sexually means being open to all aspects of our sexual selves.

1. **Eroticism in our relationship allows us to see what turns us on.** It allows us to be more fully expressive and vulnerable, sharing our sexual fantasies free of judgment.

2. **Play gives us permission to use our imagination, even pretend.** Role-playing for example is arousing and it allows us to expand our often-narrow definition of who we think we are.

3. **Heart-centered sex is about lifting and using sex to give and receive loving energy.** In heart-centered sex, we come from our most compassionate places with the intent of making our partner feel cherished, nourished and loved.

Often when a relationship is getting sexually boring, it is because it has become too unbalanced among these three areas. In a sexy marriage, there is room for all three of these aspects of our relationships and ourselves.

Where is there room for growth in your relationship in any of these three areas?

Tip 40

Write down where you are out of balance sexually with your partner. Be non-judgmental; we can all grow in this area. Then write down som ideas in how you can build up the less developed areas of your sexuality.

Tip 41
Face a fear this weekend.

What are you afraid of?

Rejection? Then ask for something so that you may possibly be rejected.

Playing sports and looking bad? Go shoot hoops with your partner (or anybody else for that matter)

Being judged for how you look? Then wear some scantily clad outfit or one that makes you stand out and get attention.

Decide that you are stronger than your fear and act accordingly! This way of living brings dividends to your life and relationships.

Tip 41

Write down a few fears and how you will lean into them rather than avoid them this week.

Tip 42
What are you sad about in your life?
What would you like to change?

Be vulnerable with your partner and allow your partner to be there for you. If your partner is not being sensitive and understanding, point it out gently and ask him to be there for you again.

If your relationship does not feel safe enough for you to be vulnerable, it may be time for some intervention. Give me a call or email me at Todd@toddcreager.com, a good relationship therapist might be just what you need to get yourself and your relationship back on track!

Tip 42

What are you willing to share with your partner this week so that you might feel more "taken care of?" Once you share with your partner, write down how that experience was for you; hopefully it was positive but if not, write that down as well.

52 Ways to Ignite Your Relationship

Tip 43
Money and Relationship Bliss

Money is an issue for all couples whether or not you talk about it. The way couples deal with money often is indicative of the overall dynamics in the relationship.

If a partner seems to control all the money, this is not just about money. This could hint at some possible relationships dynamics and issues.

Advice gathered from my experience with thousands of couples:

1. **Communicate about your money wishes and concerns.** Let your partner know how you want each person to have access to the money and how it should be spent.
2. **Have a joint account for vacations and leisure** that you both can deposit money into. Communicate and negotiate if you want to take money out.
3. **Decide on the amount that constitutes a major purchase** which means you do not act unilaterally on a purchase.
4. **If you want to spend on a major purchase, DO NOT do it secretly** to avoid a "no" or a confrontation with your partner. This is betrayal just like infidelity.
5. **If one partner is mainly responsible for managing the finances, the other needs to be involved as well,** even if it's just knowing the system the "Managing" partner is using.
6. **Be aware of the way money was or was not dealt with in your family and understand the same of your partner.** Then find YOUR way that works best for both parties.
7. **Seek to understand your partner's relationship to money and what it means to him or him or her.**

Tip 43

Write about your money relationship with your partner. Look at the 7 points above and write how these 7 ideas relate to your relationship. Also write about a few steps you can take to make changes in needed areas of your money relationship.

Tip 44
Money and the Four Temperaments

I have studied the Myers - Briggs Personality Inventory for years and utilized it in my practice. In this tip, I am relating "money" to the 4 temperaments which is a key concept.

1. **"Catalysts" have core needs of authenticity, meaning and significance.** They are motivated through their inspiration and self-actualization-focused. If they are inspired to make a purchase, they will, if the purchase gives them a sense of purpose and allows them the possibility to achieve their dreams.

2. **"Theorists" reach for mastery and control as well as knowledge and competence.** They are long-term planners, see the big picture financially and are expertise-focused. They are more apt to analyze how money is spent and create a budget that allows for success in the end.

3. **"Stabilizers" thrive when there is a sense of membership and belonging as well as when they have a reason to serve others and be dutiful.** They are security-focused and may get anxious if the financial situation seems out of control or not adding up.

4. **"Improvisers" want the freedom to act-NOW and the ability to make an impact.** They are action-focused. An improviser who loves to ski may spend money on ski equipment even if it is more than they have, because their energy comes alive when they are doing something they love.

No temperament is better or worse than another. The key is to understand and not judge your partner whose money temperament is likely different than yours.

Being able to **understand, accept and negotiate are the keys to being effective partners - financially and otherwise.**

Tip 44

From the brief descriptions above, take an educated guess about what temperaments you and your partner might be. Write down why you believe you and your partner are those particular temperaments. You might want to have your partner work with you jointly on this one. Then work towards understanding each other more and recognize the need for negotiation around money issues.

Tip 45
Co-parenting & Showing a United Front

If you have children, you may have heard that it is important to have a united front.

It's true! It is better to go along with your spouse even if you disagree than to correct her (or him) in front of the kids.

You can always pull your spouse aside away from children and state your case but the kids need to see you united. Even if you think it is good for your kids to do it your way; even if you think your spouse is way off, the benefits of having parents with a united front outweighs the disadvantages of doing it your spouse's way (no matter how much you disagree).

Of course if there is abuse, that is a different story and kids do need protection. Children who have parents who present with a united front may be frustrated because they cannot divide and conquer, but they are also more secure and relaxed.

Tip 45

What are those trigger points in you that make it difficult to keep a united front with your partner when dealing with your children? Become aware of them and have a mature conversation with your partner about these trigger points. Write down what each of you re planning to do to handle those situations better in the future.

Tip 46
Live with gratitude especially looking for reasons to be grateful for your partner.

I would suggest that this weekend you make a list of everything you are grateful for regarding your partner. For extra credit, list everything else you can think of that you appreciate.

There is nothing more powerfully positive than spending time in the energy of gratitude.

Tip 46

Write down the things you are appreciative about regarding your partner as well as anything else you can appreciate.

Tip 47
Let this be slow down and cuddle weekend.

Take your time and enjoy each other. If you are not in the habit of slowing down and touching, **start THIS WEEKEND.**

Take your partner in, receive his or her touch. Put aside any resentments, fears or any other resistance you may have. Remember the times when you did do that with your partner.

Renew and refresh that feeling with each other.

Tip 47

First, if you have any resistances to this suggestion, write about them here. See if you can process them and let them go. Then after you slow down and have some cuddling time with your partner, feel free to write about those experiences.

Tip 48
This weekend, do something for your growth.

Read a book on personal growth or relationship building. Go to a good lecture or sermon. Take a meditation class. Do something that nourishes your mind, body and soul. We are never too old to develop emotionally and psychologically.

Go deeper into yourself. Honor your soul.

Tip 48

What books are on your list? Or what else might you do in hopefully the VERY near future? Jot down a few thoughts here and then FOLLOW THROUGH! You're worth it!

Tip 49
Let this be massage weekend.

Take turns giving each other a loving, attentive massage from head to toe. Get some massage oil and find a good place to do it. Maybe you could even rent a massage table. There are even classes these days where professional massage therapists teach you how to massage each other. If you are interested in that, I have several referrals for you. That is optional though.

Enjoy giving and receiving massage even if you have never done this activity with your spouse before.

Tip 49

Describe how it was to have that mutual massage. Write down what you liked and did not like and what might you both do different in future massage dates.

Tip 50
Celebrate and Embrace Your Body

Body image, how you view and feel about your body is an important aspect of your life whether you are single or in a committed relationship. Society has put forth its own versions of what is acceptable or not and what is attractive or not.

Remember this: take care of yourself, eat well, exercise and practice good self care and hygiene. This is for YOU and your motivation should be your own health and well-being.

Where lines become crossed is when we allow our internal critic to judge. I have had many clients in my office say they can only have sex in the dark or take their clothes off under the sheets - this is no way to live and no way to have intimacy.

Embrace your body; its shape, your face. If you hide your body, you add fuel to your own inner judge. If you have a partner that is a perfectionist, then suggest that he gets some therapeutic help to see what is underlying HIS inner critic, which is then taken out on you.

Be sure to do everything you can to take care of yourself and to feel good. Your job is to embrace your body. Take your clothes off in front of your partner; make love with the lights on (at least some of the time).

Tip 50

What are areas of your body that you are critical of? How do these judgments interfere with your love life? Write down firm declarative sentences affirming your newfound "radical self-acceptance" of these parts of your body. Begin the process of letting go of the negative thoughts about your body that you cling to. They are just thoughts!

Tip 51
Use the weekend to
go further out on a limb than ever before.

Time to get a little out there this weekend...

Have fun with this: Create a song for your lover. It could be short; write down some lyrics that are romantic, loving and/or appreciative and put some music to it. The music could be either your own original score (could be the start of a new career for you) or find some other song you already like and match your lyrics to the music. Rehearse it a bit and perform if for her by Sunday night. (You don't even have to tell her or him it is my idea).

Here is a variation on that theme...

I did this for my wife many years ago: Go to a karaoke place and see if there is a way they could record you doing some love songs for your partner. You or the studio could easily burn a cd and give it to her or him as a gift. I did that and it was great; my voice was not near as good as I thought it was (actually I was pretty bad!) and my wife and I had a few good laughs. My attempt at singing her a love song had a positive effect on her and she really loved the effort!

Tip 51

Write some lyrics down here. Have fun with this even if this is a big stretch for you!

Tip 52
This weekend, splurge on a real romantic date.

Find a restaurant that is really set up for intimacy. Of course, splurging does not necessarily mean with money. (not saying that there is anything wrong with splurging with money). You can also splurge (or be generous) with your energy. Here are couple of suggestions:

- Take a nice romantic walk under the moonlight at the beach.
- Or find a lovely place in nature that is off the beaten path where you focus on each other enjoying each other and the scenery. (This could be during daylight of course. I don't want you to be on a treacherous mountain path at night and then end up MIA!)

Just make it special.

Creating an ambiance that suggests that you cherish your partner is the key. Pay attention to the mood you create or the mood that is created by the special place you take her (or him).

Celebrate your relationship! Don't wait for it to get better. Celebrate it and it WILL get better.

Tip 52

Write down what you plan on initiating. How will you set up the ambience whether it is with your words or something else that will lift your partner's energy?

About the Author

Todd Creager is a marriage and sex therapist who helps couples create loving and passionate long-term relationships. He has a talent for helping people become motivated to create new patterns in their lives that lead to more satisfying relationships and experiences. He is the author of "The Long, Hot Marriage.," a highly endorsed and regarded book for couples. He has a private practice in Huntington Beach, CA and has been helping couples and individuals for 31 years. He also does private retreats for couples committed to have the relationship they truly want.

He has been a guest as a relationship expert on many radio and TV shows including the FOX Morning News, KCAL 9 in LA, Playboy Radio, and was a therapist on Oprah Winfrey's show, "Unfaithful. " Lastly, he is an instructor at the USC School of Social Work, helping graduate students learn the theory and practice of becoming professional therapists.

Learn more about Todd Creager and get your Book Bonus at: http://toddcreager.com/bookbonus

www.ingramcontent.com/pod-product-compliance
Lightning Source LLC
Chambersburg PA
CBHW051951290426
44110CB00015B/2203